VITI

RICHARD ULACK
University of Kentucky

THE AMERICAN GEOGRAPHICAL SOCIETY
Around the World Program
HILARY LAMBERT HOPPER
University of Kentucky
Series Editor

The McDonald & Woodward Publishing Company
Blacksburg, Virginia
1995

The McDonald & Woodward Publishing Company
P. O. Box 10308, Blacksburg, Virginia 24062-0308

THE AMERICAN GEOGRAPHICAL SOCIETY
Around the World Program

Fiji

© 1995 by The American Geographical Society
The American Geographical Society is the oldest professional geographical society in the United States and a recognized pioneer in geographical research and education.

All rights reserved. First printing, 1995
Printed in Canada by DWFriesen

01 00 99 98 97 96 95   10 9 8 7 6 5 4 3 2 1

Library of Congress Cataloging-in-Publication Data

Ulack, Richard, 1942–
    Fiji / Richard Ulack.
        p.   cm. — (The American Geographical Society Around the World Program)
    Includes bibliographical references.
    ISBN 0-939923-49-1 (pbk.) : $12.95. — ISBN 0-939923-50-5 (library) : $17.95
    1. Fiji. I. Title. II. Series: American Geographical Society Around the World Program (Series)
DU600.U47 1995
916.11—dc20   94-4368
                                                                                                   C

Cover: Women assembling for a *meke* for tourists on Ono-i-lau Island, Fiji. *Meke* and other traditions of the islands are important components of Fiji's growing tourism industry. Photograph by Ralph E. Eshelman of Lusby, Maryland.

All original sketches by Jennifer Snow.

Photo credits: Ralph E. Eshelman (pp. 8, 17, 18, 23, 25, 29, 30, 37, 38, 50, 52, 53, 55); Fiji Visitors Bureau (p. 43); Richard Ulack (pp. 10, 14, 15, 26, 28, 31, 34, 36, 42, 57).

Base for maps on pp. iv and 45 by Center for Cartography and Geographic Information, University of Kentucky.

For additional information about the Around the World Program, please contact the publisher.

TABLE OF CONTENTS

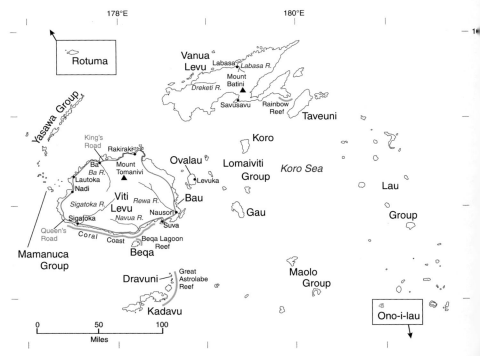

The Fiji Islands and their place in the South Pacific Island Region. Fiji comprises more t
three hundred islands, most of them small and uninhabited.
Only the major islands are shown on this map.

FIJI

VITI

ijians are an intelligent, sophisticated people accustomed to long-distance ocean travel in small boats. ...avel by boat to and from their islands ...ade the Fijians familiar with differing ...man customs that had developed on ...eir many islands, those of neighbor... Tonga and Samoa, and beyond. ...d, since the mid-1600s, Western ...ing ships had been sighted passing ...r or through the Fiji Islands. The ...iting moments of Fijian history are ...served as *mekes* — saga-length

dances accompanied by songs and the beating of drums.

In 1800, the American ship *Argo* wrecked off the island of Oneata and, in the following year, the badly-damaged Spanish vessel *El Plumier* limped into Bua Bay on the west side of Vanua Levu to make repairs. Events unfolding from both arrivals have been preserved in mekes. Survivors of the *Argo* were at first mistaken for gods. According to the meke *Nukuthainga* ("The Place of Blown Sand"):

Two Levuka men were sent to see [the wrecked ship] and saw what appeared to be men, but [the Levuka men] thought they must be gods, as they were biting live fire and had their ears wrapped up. This was because they had never before seen pipes smoked nor the red caps the men were wearing.

The American sailors also introduced tobacco, Western diseases, and fire-arms to the islands. The firearms were used both conventionally and unconventionally. According to *Nukuthainga:*

Some old men of Oneata hid some casks of gunpowder, to use as black paints for their bodies, and some ramrods to use as scratchers for their heads.

A three-tailed comet was visible in the skies over Fiji for thirty-seven days in 1800, during which time the *Argo* wrecked. That comet, the unusual co-incidence of two disabled Western ships appearing over such a short period of two years, and the new ideas, objects, and diseases brought by the Westerners all were taken as super-natural signs of coming change. Indeed, a survivor of the *Argo* was rescued by *El Plumier,* and that survivor spread word of the valuable sandal-wood — a rare source of scent for perfume — growing on the islands. Soon, the portent of change sensed by the Fijians became a reality as Bua Bay became world-famous as Sandalwood Bay, and the Fiji — or Sandalwood — Islands became drawn inescapably int the then-developing global network o accelerating cultural and environmen tal change.

The meke combines dance, song, and drums in a saga-length story.

THREE HUNDRED TINY ISLANDS

The Pacific Ocean is by far the largest of the world's oceans; it is more than twice the size of the Atlantic Ocean and covers more of the globe's surface than all the land areas combined. The Pacific Island region — called Oceania when Australia and New Zealand are included — is made up of some 25,000 islands, islets, and atolls, most of which are too small to support permanent human settlement. The Pacific Island region is divided into three subregions: Polynesia, Micronesia, and Melanesia. The name of each subregion reveals something of its nature: *poly* refers to the many islands in the vast expanse covered by Polynesia; *micro* suggests the tiny size of the islands of Micronesia; and *mela* refers to the black skin pigmentation of native people of Melanesia. Fiji is located in the South Pacific Ocean and is part of Melanesia, but its location on the eastern edge of that subregion, close to Polynesia, explains why some of its cultural characteristics are more Polynesian than Melanesian. The indigenous people of Fiji are called Fijians; they are a black-skinned, handsome people of considerably larger stature than most other Melanesians, and are well-known for their athletic prowess on the rugby field.

Today, Fiji is populated by several groups other than Fijians; these include Europeans, who first sighted Fiji in 1643 and, most importantly, Indians or, as they are sometimes called, Indo-Fijians. The Indians were brought to Fiji from India, beginning in 1879, as indentured laborers to work on the Australian-owned sugar plantations. For many years, until the late 1980s, when political turmoil caused significant emigration of Indo-Fijians, this group actually out-numbered ethnic Fijians. Fiji today is one of the most culturally diverse of the South Pacific island nations.

Fiji consists of about one hundred

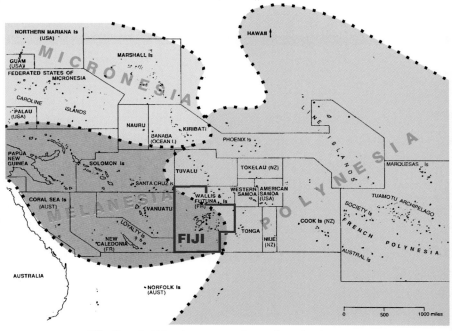

The Pacific Island region and its cultural subregions.

inhabited islands, another two hundred or so that are probably large enough to be inhabited, and additional hundreds of tiny islets, atolls, and reefs. These islands are scattered over more than one million square miles of ocean. Fiji's capital and largest city, Suva, is situated more than 2,700 miles southwest of Honolulu, 1,700 miles northeast of Sydney, Australia, and 1,300 miles north of Auckland, New Zealand. Taken together, the land area totals 7,056 square miles, an area slightly larger than the states of Hawaii or Connecticut, or a bit smaller than Massachusetts, but most of the islands are spread across an area comparable to that of Illinois. There are several outlying islands; all islands in the country occupy an area about twice the size of Texas. The two largest islands, Viti Levu and Vanua Levu, account for more than eighty-seven percent of the nation's total land area; these two islands, together with the five next largest, represent ninety-five percent of total land area of the country.

While Fiji is small compared to m

POLITICAL UNITS OF THE PACIFIC
POLITICAL STATUS, AREA, POPULATION AND DENSITY, 1988–1991[1]

Political Unit	Political Status[2]	Area (square miles)	Population (number)	Population (per square mile)
Melanesia				
Fiji	1 (1970)	7,056	746,326	105
New Caledonia (FR)	3 (1956)	7,172	164,173	22
Papua-New Guinea	1 (1975)	178,260	3,529,538	20
Solomon Islands	1 (1978)	10,985	318,707	30
Vanuatu	1 (1980)	5,700	147,000	26
Micronesia				
Federated States of Micronesia (US)	2 (1986)	271	100,000	369
Guam (US)	3 (1898)	209	133,152	637
Kiribati	1 (1979)	277	72,298	261
Marshall Islands (US)	2 (1986)	70	43,355	619
Nauru	1 (1968)	8	9,350	1,168
Northern Mariana Islands (US)	3 (1986)	184	43,345	236
Trust Territory of the Pacific: Palau (US)	3 (1947)	458	15,105	33
Polynesia				
American Samoa (US)	3 (1899)	77	46,800	608
Cook Islands (NZ)	2 (1965)	93	19,000	204
Easter Island (Chile)	3 (1888)	47	2,100	45
French Polynesia (FR)	3 (1946)	1,359	199,031	146
Hawaii (US state)	Statehood (1959)	6,471	1,108,229	171
Niue (NZ)	2 (1965)	101	2,267	22
Tokelau (NZ)	3 (1948)	4	1,690	422
Tonga	1 (1970)	270	90,485	335
Tuvalu	1 (1978)	10	8,229	823
Wallis & Futuna Islands (FR)	3 (1961)	106	13,705	129
Western Samoa	1 (1962)	1,093	159,862	146
Total		220,281	6,973,747	32
Total (excluding Papua-New Guinea and Hawaii)		35,550	2,335,980	66

Population figures are official estimates or census figures for years 1988–1991.
Political status and year that status was attained is given. Units with "1" are politically inde-
pendent; "2" indicates units that are internally self-governing or in "free association" with
former colonial power; "3" indicates colonies with some lesser degree of autonomy.
Sources: *National Geographic Atlas of the World*, National Geographic Society, 1992; *The Far
East and Australia*, Europa Publications, 1992.

continental nations, the country is among the largest of the political entities that make up the Pacific Island region. Only the independent nations of Papua-New Guinea and Solomon Islands and the French territory of New Caledonia are larger. In terms of population, only Papua-New Guinea has more people than does Fiji. Fiji's nearest neighbors are the independent nations of Western Samoa and Tonga to the east, Tuvalu to the north, and Vanuatu to the west.

Fiji is located at about 18° South latitude which means that it is slightly closer to the equator than Hawaii, which is located at about 20° North latitude. The 180° meridian passes through Fiji and bisects Taveuni, Fiji's third largest island. The *International Date Line* normally lies upon the 180° meridian, but

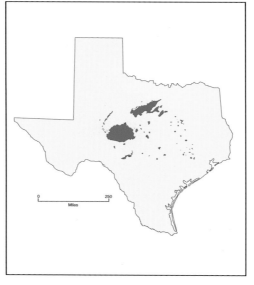

The two largest islands of Fiji occupy slightly less land than the state of Massachusetts, but the total area within the territorial waters of Fiji is nearly twice that of Texas.

Fiji is one of the places where it deviates from this meridian. By international agreement, all of the islands of Fiji are located to the west of the International Date Line in order to keep al of the islands within the same day. Th new day first appears at midnight at tl date line and advances westward around the globe until it finally "disap pears." Thus, as one travels by airplane or ship from, say, Tahit: California, or H waii to Fiji — tl is, from east to west — the dat becomes one da "later" as one crosses the date line. For this re son the masthe of the country' major daily ne paper, *The Fiji Times*, accurat states that it is "The First Newspape Read in the World Today."

The next largest islands after Viti Levu and Vanua Levu are Taveuni adavu, the latter pronounced Kandavu." Other, smaller islands inlude Beqa ("Benka"), the home of the ijian firewalkers; Rabi ("Rambi"), day the home of a Polynesian group hich immigrated from Banaba (Ocean land); and Rotuma, a Polynesian utlier" located some two-hundredty miles north of Suva. The smaller ands and islets of Fiji can be placed to several island groups including the maiviti ("middle," or central) group; e Lau group in eastern Fiji, which n be further subdivided into Northn, Central, and Southern Lau; the ala group, located between Kadavu d Southern Lau; the Yasawa group, ated to the northwest of Viti Levu; the Mamanuca ("Mamanutha") up, located immediately offshore n Nadi ("Nandi") in western Viti u, the location of Fiji's internaal airport. Western Viti Levu and Mamanucas, though very small ds, are well-known because of r popular tourist resorts. The aiviti group includes Fiji's fifth, h, and seventh largest islands — , Koro, and Ovalau, respectively. small town of Levuka, on Ovalau,

was the site of the first European settlement in the Fiji Islands and at one time the colonial capital of Fiji.

Fiji's rugged, beautiful landscape is of volcanic origin. The island group is located astride the *Ring of Fire,* the boundary between the Pacific and the Indo-Australian plates. Here, the Indo-Australian plate slowly disappears beneath the Pacific plate along what is called a subduction zone. It is in such zones that most of the world's earthquakes and volcanic eruptions, or tectonic activities, occur. Fiji, fortunately, has not been devastated in recent times by tectonic activity.

The larger islands of Fiji generally have narrow, sometimes densely-populated coastal plains with spectacular mountains rising abruptly from the coast. For example, only fifteen percent of Viti Levu is in lowlands. The highest point on Fiji is Mount Tomanivi which rises to 4,341 feet above sea level on Viti Levu. During the colonial period Mount Tomanivi was called Mount Victoria after Queen Victoria. A rugged divide running generally from north to south forms a physical boundary that roughly splits Viti Levu into an

The rugged east or windward shore of Dravuni Island clearly shows the dark volcanic rock that makes up the high islands of Fiji.

southern part of the divide important peaks include Mount Monavatu and Mount Tuvutau (formerly Mount Gordon, named after Fiji's first British colonial governor). Fiji's largest river, the Rewa, flows southeastward from its origin in the highlands east of the divide. The delta of the Rewa, located south of the city of Nausori, is very wide. Viti Levu's other major rivers are the Navua, also on the eastern side of the divide, and the Sigatoka and Mba (or Ba), both of which originate in the highlands on the western side of the divide. Because Viti Levu's rivers fre

eastern and western half. Mount Tomanivi marks the northern extension of this divide. To the south are a number of other peaks in excess of three thousand feet and several high plateaus, including the Nadrau Plateau in the central part of the island. In the

The more placid west or leeward shore of Dravuni Island contains a beach washed by quiet waters.

uently tumble rapidly downslope,
here are many waterfalls and rapids.
Whitewater rafting is a tourist activity
in some areas, notably on the upper
reaches of the Navua River. The valley
of the Sigatoka River, which meets the
sea near the coastal town of Sigatoka,
is very important agriculturally, for
there is grown a wide variety of cash
crops sold in urban marketplaces all
over Viti Levu. Because of the variety
of vegetables grown in this area, it is
called Fiji's "salad bowl." Boat rides
on river are available for visitors who
want to see Fiji's spectacular interiors.
One can, for example, take a motor-
boat ride from the city of Navua, on
the south coast of the island, up the
Navua River to the interior village of
Namuamua where the tourist is introduced to the rural Fijian village way of
life. Numerous small villages dot the
interior uplands of Viti Levu and the
other larger islands of Fiji. Nearly all of
the residents of these upland villages are
ethnic Fijians.

High volcanic mountains and plateaus also characterize the other larger
islands of Fiji. Vanua Levu, the second
largest island, has a number of eleva-

tions above three thousand feet in its
central spine, which runs generally
from east to west. The highest point,
3,386 feet, is located in the center of
the island about half-way between
Vanua Levu's two major towns, Labasa
on the north coast and Savusavu on
the south coast. Mount Navotuvoto,
2,764 feet, is located near the western
end of the island; this peak is a good
example of a shield volcano — a volcano built up over time by layer-upon-
layer of flowing lava. Except for an area
along the northwest coast where
Vanua Levu's largest river, the Dreketi,
drains into the sea, the coastal plain is
narrow, a circumstance that limits agricultural productivity. The eastern portion of Vanua Levu consists of two
peninsulas separated by Natewa Bay.

Fiji's third largest island, Taveuni, is
located southeast of Vanua Levu across
the Somosomo Strait. Taveuni, con-
taining only 181 square miles, is less
than one-tenth the size of Vanua Levu
which, in turn, is only one-half the size
of Viti Levu. Many agree that Taveuni
is the most scenic of Fiji's islands because of its rugged beauty — its highest
peak, at 4,072 feet, is the second high-

The rugged interior of Viti Levu shows the mountainous landscape, evergreen forest, and rain-bearing clouds that are typical of the large island of Fiji. The village of Lutu lies in the clearing.

est mountain in the nation — and its lush natural vegetation and native fauna which have been disturbed less by humans than that on the larger islands. Taveuni's bird life is especially noteworthy and several rare, endemic species attract birdwatchers to the island. Taveuni is the only one of Fiji's larger islands to be free of the notorious exotic pest — the mongoose — which means that birds on the island have not suffered because of the mongoose's appetite for eggs. A number of fringing coral reefs around Taveuni and nearby Vanua Levu also make these islands very attractive for scuba divers. Indeed, the Rainbow Reef's White Wall is one of a number of dive sites in Fiji that are considered to be among the best in the world.

Similar to Taveuni in size and scenic beauty is Kadavu Island, 158 square miles in area, located about fifty-five miles south of Viti Levu. Like all of Fiji's smaller islands, the population c Kadavu is almost entirely native Fijia This island, which is off the beaten track and therefore not often visited many tourists, is noted for its traditional Fijian culture. Also like Taveu Kadavu has world class scuba diving sites associated with the Great Astro labe Reef, one of the finest barrier re in the world.

Fiji has a tropical maritime climat climate that is heavily influenced by the prevailing southeast trade winds and that is generally hot and humid throughout the year. The seasonal s of prevailing winds, the mediating e fects of the ocean, and the topograp features of the larger islands, howev

THE GREAT ASTROLABE REEF,
CHARLES DARWIN, AND ATOLLS

The Great Astrolabe Reef provides excellent support for the 19th-century evolutionary biologist Charles Darwin's theory of the formation of atolls, or "low islands." An atoll is an island made up of coralline formations (limestone), usually in the shape of an irregular ring around a lagoon. Usually the ring is "broken" into pieces, called *motus*, which are separated by channels connecting the surrounding ocean and the central lagoon. Darwin theorized that as high volcanic islands erode they subside into the sea; the original islands' fringing and/or barrier reefs eventually become the atoll as the volcanic portion ultimately, and very slowly over geologic time, sinks beneath the sea. A coral atoll or reef can, therefore, indicate the size of a former volcanic "high island." The vast majority of Pacific low islands and atolls are quite small, most are very dry and lack drinking water, and the coralline-derived soils are infertile. As a result, permanent human settlement and commercial agriculture are not feasible. Such islands are often pictured in advertisements and movies with pristine beaches and waving coconut palms, a trademark image of idyllic South Sea islands. While the scenic beauty of such islands is real, life in such a setting is often difficult because of very limited supplies of critical natural resources.

Overall, Fiji comprises several hundred islands, most of which are atolls and most of which are either not populated or have very small populations of humans.

produce some important climatic
erences within the country. Sum-
, from November to about March,
ne hottest and wettest part of the
r; the period from June until Sep-
ber is cooler and drier.

is the eastern, especially the southern, or windward coasts of Fiji's
er islands that receive the greatest

amounts of rainfall whereas the leeward, or western, sides receive less.
Characteristic of most tropical cli-
mates, Fiji's average annual lowland
temperature is hot, about 77°F. At
Suva, the monthly average ranges from
about 73°F in July to a high of 81°F in
February, the summer's hottest and
most humid month. Rainfall amounts

AVERAGE ANNUAL TEMPERATURE AND RAINFALL
FOR SUVA AND NADI

	Suva		Nadi	
	Temperature (degrees F)	Rainfall (inches)	Temperature (degrees F)	Rainfall (inches)
January	80.2	12.2	80.6	11.5
February	80.4	11.7	80.4	11.3
March	80.2	15.1	80.1	14.5
April	79	13.4	79.2	7.6
May	76.6	10.9	77	3.9
June	75	6.9	75.2	3
July	73.6	5.8	73.9	2
August	73.8	7.8	74.8	2.4
September	74.7	8.3	76.1	3.4
October	75.9	8.5	77.4	2.8
November	77.5	10.5	78.6	5.3
December	79.2	12.2	79.9	7.1
Average Temperature	77.2		77.7	
Total Annual Rainfall		123.3		74.8

vary throughout the year in Suva, and elsewhere, with the southeast trades bringing the greatest amount of rainfall in summer between November and April. Of Suva's total annual rainfall of 123 inches, over sixty percent falls during this six-month period. July, the coolest month, also has the least amount of rainfall and the lowest humidity. Viti Levu's western side, as typified by Nadi, has monthly temperature averages very similar to Suva's but the rainfall amounts differ markedly. Nadi receives only seventy-five inches every year with over seventy-five percent of the total falling from Novemb through April. July, the driest month receives less than two inches of rainfall! One might conclude that most tourists from temperate parts of the world would find the cooler months, and especially July, the most pleasan time to visit Suva. Indeed, there is a very close relationship between clim and tourist visits to Fiji. The fact tha some of Fiji's major resorts are locate on the western coast of Viti Levu an in the nearby Mamanuca Island gro

in part because this side of the island
as less clouds and rainfall and there-
ore more clear days for those who are
eking the sun.

On the larger islands, temperatures
e considerably cooler at the higher
evations in the interior. Furthermore,
the windward side of the interior
ountain ranges precipitation in-
eases significantly. As the moisture-
len air is forced to rise in elevation it
ols and thus its ability to hold mois-
re decreases, resulting in rainfall on
e mountainsides that in some places
ceeds two hundred inches annually.
e leeward, or west-facing, sides of
mountain ranges, on the other
nd, are much drier.

Natural hazards, especially cyclones
the Pacific equivalent of hurricanes
can be devastating and have from
e to time severely affected Fiji's
nomy, especially agriculture and
rism, to say nothing of loss of life
property from the storm and result-
flooding. During the last decade Fiji
suffered a greater frequency of
r cyclones than is normal. In 1985,
such storms, *Nigel* and *Eric*, re-
d in more than twenty-five deaths

and massive flooding. Coastal villages
that were most affected completely lost
their agricultural harvests for that year.
The ethnic Fijians in those villages who
depend heavily on their agricultural
output for subsistence were without
food. More recently, on January 2 and
3, 1993, Cyclone *Kina* pulverized the
eastern and southern portions of Viti
Levu, Fiji's most heavily populated
area. This storm caused more than
twenty-five deaths; huge losses of housing; hundreds of millions of dollars
worth of damage; the loss of three major bridges, including one on Queen's
Highway that crosses the Sigatoka
River at Sigatoka; and untold destruc-
tion to agriculture including the near
total loss of food crops and the loss of
ninety percent of the livestock in the
affected area, the heart of Fiji's dairy
industry. Suva, Nausori, and Navua
were especially hard hit by the storm.

The natural vegetation of the drier
western side of Viti Levu is grasslands
and scrub vegetation, while that of the
wetter eastern side is rainforest. Ap-
proximately one-half of Fiji is in forest,
most of which is on the larger "high"
islands like Viti Levu. More than three

The Sigatoka River drains much of southwestern Viti Levu. This bridge on the Queen's Highway at Sigatoka was damaged in Cyclone Kina in January, 1993.

thousand species of plant life are known to occur on Fiji; about one-third of these are endemics found *only* in Fiji. When Europeans first reached the islands, coconuts, mangrove forests along portions of the coast, bamboo, and the species-rich rainforests were much in evidence. A European visitor to this rainforest during the mid-nineteenth century reported ". . . though there was a thick wood, the actual virgin forest did not commence until we had attained the height of about 2,500 feet above the sea. When entering that region we found the trees altogether different from those of the lowlands, and densely covered with mosses, lichens, and deep orange-coloured orchids. Some of the ferns were of antediluvian dimensions. A species of

Cinnamomum, producing a superior kind of cassia-bark, and used by the natives for scenting cocoa-nut oil, an as a powerful sudorific, was met with considerable quantities. The absence all large animals, and the limited num ber of birds, impart an air of solemnit to these upland forests. Not a sound heard: all is silence – repose!"

Among the more important trees exploited during the early years of Eu ropean contact was the aromatic san dalwood, harvested on Vanua Levu the British nearly to the point of extinction. In recent years, Caribbean pines have been introduced in parts drier western Viti Levu with the goa increasing commercial lumber produ tion. The rainforests, where most pl and animal species are found, are b estroyed by commercial logging and ncreasing demands for additional farm nd.

Before the Europeans reached Fiji, nly a few species of mammals were und on the islands. Among the na- ve species were several different kinds bats and the Polynesian grey rat; mesticates included the dog and pig, ought to the islands by the first lynesian navigators who arrived from e west. A variety of land and sea ds, reptiles including snakes and anas, amphibians, and of course a mendous abundance of sea life nd out the list of animal life. Numerous animal species have been roduced in the last tury, the most famous or infamous, depend- on one's perspective of these exotics being mongoose, the mynah , and the giant toad. mongoose was intro- ed from India in the 0s to control rats ch were feeding on r cane. The mon- e has become a men-

ace because, instead of controlling rats and snakes, it has turned to chickens and native bird populations as a major source of food. The mynah bird, also imported from India, has driven many of Fiji's endemic bird species to the interior. In the populated areas of low- land Fiji one can expect to be awak- ened by the loud cackle of mynahs. The giant toad, imported from Hawaii in the 1930s to control some of the islands' larger insect pests, has become so numerous that it is difficult to avoid stepping on, or running over, them, especially at night when they are most active. The toad's major enemies are people, the automobile, and their own

The flowers of tropi- cal plants are often large, numerous, and colorful. This is the blossom of the exotic ornamental dwarf poinciana in Kula Bird Park, situated in a section of coastal rainforest east of Sigatoka.

kind as they tend to feed on each other when nothing else is available.

Except for those species that have been introduced by humans, nearly all of Fiji's land animals originated to the west. Exceptions to this may be the two species of iguana that are found on the islands, the banded iguana and the crested iguana. Iguanas are native to Central and South America, and are thought to have reached Fiji after drifting across the Pacific Ocean on large pieces of floating matter, such as vegetation. The crested iguana was only recently discovered in Fiji and so far is thought to be limited to one small island off Vanua Levu. Although Fiji has a number of land-dwelling snake species, including the Pacific boa, only one variety of venomous snake, the rare bolo, occurs on the islands. Bites from the bolo or the several species of poisonous sea snakes are rare since the snakes are quite docile.

A tremendous abundance and variety of sea life is found in the waters surrounding Fiji. Fish and shellfish are commercially important, and the beauty and bounty of the coral reefs mean that diving and snorkeling draw tourists to the country. In addition to the usual varieties of fish and shellfish that are exploited for food, one form of sea life deserves special mention because it, along with sandalwood, was one of the important natural resources exploited early on by the Europeans. *Bêche-de-mer,* more commonly known as the sea cucumber, is a rather ugly slug-like creature that is abundant in the waters of Fiji. Because it was prized as food in China, where it was known as *trepang,* collecting and processing stations were set up in Fiji to smoke and dry the animals for export. Shark — especially their fins, used by the Chinese in soups — several species of large sea turtles, and lobsters are other examples of sea life that are commercially exploited today. Although sea turtles and their eggs are protected during the "winter" nesting season by Fijian law, their populations have dwindled because they have been over-exploited for both meat and shells.

Sandalwood, and later bêche-de-mer, were important exports during years immediately following European contact. Bêche-de-mer are no longer exported but other products from the

A fisherman unloads his catch at the Princes Wharf fish market on Nabuka'lou Creek, Suva.

— most notably tuna, harvested by industry developed with Japanese — today earn export dollars. An- her natural resource that provides ort revenues is gold, mined at Vatu- la in northern Viti Levu, but the plies are limited and accessible ore uld be exhausted by about the year 0. Copper is known to exist in Fiji is not yet mined. With the excep- of hydroelectricity, Fiji has no wn energy resources and spends siderable revenues purchasing fuels. eginning in the 1960s, Fiji began to gnize the scientific and economic ortance of the islands' natural ty. The Fiji National Trust began, 981, to organize national parks to erve unspoiled areas on land and e surrounding waters, and to pro- native plants and animals, includ-

ing such endangered species as the long-legged warbler and Fiji banded iguana. The islands' scenic beauty also was developed as a tourist attraction. The volcanic landscape, pristine beaches, and coral reefs, combined with Fiji's excellent situation in the Pacific, resulted in tourism becoming the nation's leading source of foreign revenue, and today Fiji receives more tourists than any other South Pacific island nation. Because of Fiji's strategic location in the Pacific, Nadi Interna- tional Airport has been a convenient stopover for airplanes flying between North America or Hawaii and Austra- lia, New Zealand, or other, smaller Pacific nations. On the other hand, the emergence of the much larger, faster, and more far-ranging commercial jet aircraft has also meant that Fiji is often bypassed as non-stop long-distance flights are now possible. Today, no American airline has a regularly-scheduled stopover at Nadi.

Coupled with these "natural" resources has been the development of a number of commercial agricultural resources, by far the most important of which has been sugar cane. Until tourism took over first place in 1991, sugar was the leading money earner for Fiji; today it is a close second. The Fiji Sugar Corporation wants to diversify into producing ethanol as a domestic fuel. The government of Fiji has launched a five-year plan to develop the agricultural potential of Sigatoka Valley to reduce dependency upon imported foodstuffs. Copra and other coconut products and those of the re-

Diving Fiji's reefs is a major tourist activi

cently-established pine and hardwood plantations are among the other important commercial products of Fiji toda. British Petroleum Ltd. and the Fiji P Commission have worked together to produce pine chips for export to Japa and sawn hardwood to Australia. Fiji hopes to eventually quadruple the income it presently receives for timber products.

Copra is dried coconut. Here, sun-dried copra is being prepared on the island of Ono-i-lau.

PEOPLING THE EASTERN FRONTIER

OF MELANESIA

As is true of nearly all life on the islands of the western Pacific Ocean, the first humans to reach Fiji originated in southeastern Asia. From the Malay Peninsula and Indonesian archipelago, humans traveled to New Guinea, Australia, and, ultimately, throughout the thousands of Pacific islands. Although experts don't completely agree on the details, archeological evidence strongly suggests that the islands of Fiji were settled by several different waves of immigrants who came by way of islands to the west that included New Britain and the Solomons. The first wave — light-skinned ancestors of the present-day Polynesians — arrived at least 3,500 years ago brought with them a diversity of plants that included the taro root, their major subsistence crop, now called *dalo* in Fiji; pigs; and a culture associated with a distinctive style of pottery called Lapita as well as tools and ornaments made from shells.

Lapita pottery, decorated in horizontal bands, has been found at archeological sites near Sigatoka. The Lapita culture, comprising sophisticated seafarers and horticulturists who brought to the places they settled their Austronesian (or Malay-Polynesian) languages, diffused eastward to Tonga, Samoa, and beyond. Today, about six hundred different Austronesian languages are spoken throughout the Pacific region and in much of Southeast Asia. Fijian is one such Austronesian language and there are a number of distinctive dialects spoken.

Later, waves of seafarers also came from the western Melanesian islands. These more recent immigrants were dark-skinned and culturally Melanesian, and they brought their own distinctive cultural traditions.

Because Fiji is situated near the boundary between the culture regions of Polynesia and Melanesia, there has been considerable contact and interac-

THE FIJIAN LANGUAGE

Fijian, which comprises a number of dialects and belongs to the Malay-Polynesian, or Austronesian, family of languages, originated in Southeast Asia. Other languages in the Malay-Polynesian family include Malay, Hawaiian, Maori, Tongan, and Rotuman — the language of a Polynesian group living on Rotuma, a small island that is part of Fiji. Languages in the same family, of course, share many similarities. The word for fish, for example, is *ika* in Fijian, Tongan, or Maori; *ikan* in Malay; and *i'a* in Hawaiian and Rotuman.

In the 1830s, two Wesleyan missionaries, David Cargill and William Cross, devised a spelling and writing system for Fijian. From among the many and varied Fijian dialects found throughout the islands, the missionaries selected Bauan to be the basis for the official version of Fijian. Bau ("Mbau") was the political center of Fiji at the time. In 1850, a dictionary was published and, soon after, the Bible was translated into Fijian.

Many Fijian words are pronounced differently than would be expected by one who speaks English. The island name Kadavu is, for example, is pronounced "Kandavu." The missionaries developed a system based on simplicity, regularity, and the ease with which the writing system could be used by the Fijians who were learning it. One difference between the spoken and written versions of the language, for example, is that in Fijian speech all consonants are separated by a vowel. In the spoken Fijian language some words include consonants that sound like *mb, nd, ng,* and *th.* When Cargill included these consonants in the written form, his Fijian students would pronounce them with a separating vowel. The written word *Kandavu,* for example, would be pronounced *Kan-a-da-vu* in conformance with the vowel rule. In the words of Cargill, "we therefore substituted one consonant for two, and the natives were quite delighted with the improvement, and joyfully exclaimed, 'You have just now known the nature of our language; we are just now able to read the books which you have written'." Thus, the letter *b* came to represent *mb, d* represents *nd, q* represents *ng+g* (as in finger), *g* represents *ng* (as in singer), and *c* represents *th* (as in father). Most of the other consonants are similar, except for some pronunciations, to their English counterparts; the vowels are also similar.

A visitor to Fiji should know a few useful phrases. *Bula* literally means "health," or "life," and in everyday conversation, "hello," or "how are you?;" *Ni sa moce* ("mothe") means "good night," or "good-bye;" *Vinaka* means "good," or "thank you;" and *Vinaka vaka-levu* means "thank you very much" (after Schütz 1979).

on between Fiji and Polynesian ⌐onga in the period since both have ⌐en settled. Intermarriage, especially ⌐tween Tongans and Fijians from ⌐i's easternmost Lau Island group, ⌐ans that Fijians from Lau are physi-⌐lly distinct from their more western ⌐ighbors. In short, racially and cultur-⌐y, Fijians represent more of a mix ⌐tween Polynesia and Melanesia than ⌐other Pacific peoples because of the ⌐ation of the islands. Some have said ⌐t Fijians are racially more similar to ⌐lanesians but culturally more like ⌐ynesians. One important example of ⌐olynesian tradition is that Fijian ⌐iety is hierarchical, with tribal ⌐ups led by chiefs. Tribes are divided

into clans, called *mataqali* in Fijian, and each village has its own subclans. Each clan has its own function — there are, for example, chiefly clans, military clans, and clans of various kinds of workers, such as fishermen. Throughout Fiji's history such tribes have formed confederations which were led by paramount chiefs. Confederations were formed through alliances or conquests, the latter resulting from the frequent wars that took place.

The hostilities among Fijians led to the development of traditional settlements that were defense oriented. Villages were often located in the delta swamplands and surrounded with fences, ditches, and concealed and

Bau Village, the capital of Fiji before the islands became a British colony, was a model for other coastal villages of the islands.

upraised spikes. Styled after the center of power on Bau, villages included a special temple to the ancestral god of the main chiefs, rock-lined platforms for the houses of leaders, and stone-bordered canoe docks. Additional land was created by filling in the shoreline and constructing terraces.

One pre-Christian cultural characteristic found throughout most of Fiji was the practice of cannibalism, which in Fiji began more than two thousand years ago. Cannibalism was an intrinsic part of Fijian religion. Victims were nearly always those taken as a result of wars and the defeated could expect to become human sacrifices required by the great warrior gods. Eating the vanquished was to bestow the ultimate disgrace upon them, and in the religious system which included ancestor worship, such a practice was a lasting insult to the family of the victim. Other related practices included the killing of wives of chiefs who died so that they could follow their husbands into the next world, and the preservation of human skulls for use in drinking *yaqona*, a traditional beverage of Fiji. The arrival of Europeans and Christian

missionaries, and the subsequent conversion of Fijians to Christianity, brought about the disappearance of cannibalism from most of Fiji during the first half of the nineteenth centur By the latter half of the 1800s there were a few groups still practicing cann balism in some of the more remote in terior regions of the largest islands. It said that a European missionary, Rev erend Thomas Baker, was eaten in th central part of Viti Levu as late as 1867. Today, Fijians abhor cannibalism.

Abel Tasman, in charge of two ves sels which belonged to the Dutch Ea India Company, passed within sight Taveuni in 1643. Tasman, for whom the Australian island and state of T mania were named, was also the firs European navigator to see New Zealand, Tonga, and Tasmania. Otl famous European navigators to pass through the Fijian islands were Cap James Cook, who sailed through the southern part of the Lau group duri his second voyage in the Pacific in 1774, and Captain William Bligh. F passed through the heart of the Fiji group in 1789 in a small, open long

YAQONA

Yaqona, pronounced "yangona" in Fijian and called *kava* in most of the Pacific, is the traditional island drink made from roots of *Piper methysticum*, a member of the pepper family. In preparing yaqona, the roots are crushed, then the fluid is squeezed and strained into the large yaqona bowl, called a *tanoa*. Water or coconut milk is added, the mixture is stirred, any woody material is removed, and the beverage is ready to drink as part of a ceremonial feast. The national drink of Fiji, yaqona is non-alcoholic but has an euphoric effect on those (typically men) who partake in the ancient custom of (usually) sitting on a woven floor mat around a tanoa, and drinking a liquid that looks and tastes very unusual to the uninitiated — and may take some time to get used to! Yaqona is a muddy-looking liquid that today is drunk from cups made from the hard shell of coconuts.

Yaqona fluid being squeezed from the pepper root into the tanoa as part of the Yaqona ceremony.

ch he and a few loyal officers sailed r the mutiny that took place in gan waters on HMS *Bounty*. Bligh's was to sail west to the distant Por- ese colony of Timor in the Indone- archipelago. He sailed through t European navigators of the time d the "Cannibal Islands" and was ast once pursued by hostile Fijians eir war canoes as he passed be-

tween Viti Levu and Vanua Levu. After nearly six weeks Bligh, who kept a careful diary of his adventures, eventually landed in Timor. Since Tasman and Cook only skirted the perimeter of Fiji's islands, it was really the unwilling Bligh who was the first European explorer to give an accurate description of the island group. Both Cook and Bligh returned to the Fijian islands in

Fijian men visiting the ship H.M.S. Providence, *commanded by Captain William Bligh on his return to the islands in 1792.*

later voyages.

American sailors also visited Fiji. In 1834, the entire crew of an American merchant ship, the *Charles Dogett,* was killed by Fijians in southeastern Viti Levu. In 1840, an American expedition led by Commodore Charles Wilkes carefully explored and mapped the islands. In addition to charting the islands, Wilkes sought revenge for the massacre of the *Dogett* crew and in so doing he captured and took to the United States the Fijian who had been in charge of the earlier massacre. Wilkes, who severely punished other Fijians for what to him were misdeeds, was court-martialed for his harsh treat-

ment of Fijians but was eventually cleared of all charges.

Because dangerous reefs made sail Fijian waters very hazardous, and be cause Fijians were perceived as fierc cannibalistic people, the islands wer not settled by Westerners until the 1800s. The first significant Western settlement took place in the first de cade of the nineteenth century on t western side of Vanua Levu, in the coastal area of Bua Bay, once sanda wood was discovered by the surviv the *Argo* shipwreck. As word got ou many others arrived to seek their fc tunes from sandalwood. Sandalwoo the name given to several fragrant

opical trees, but especially *Santalum*
bum, an evergreen, partly parasitic
ee. The wood was carved ornamen-
lly and the oil was (and still is) dis-
led for use in perfumes and incense.
 exchange for their sandalwood, the
ians received European-made wares
ch as nails, tools, whales' teeth
lled *tabua* in Fijian, a valuable gift
d token of respect), and, eventually,
ns. Vanua Levu came to be called
ndalwood Island by early European
d American traders and many
achcombers," early European pio-
rs, settled in Fiji. By 1820, sandal-
od was scarce. Ships that had once
en aboard cargoes of several hun-
d tons had to settle for several hun-
d pounds.
ollowing the demise of the sandal-

wood trade, the beachcombers were
hired as mercenaries, or paid soldiers,
by Fijian chiefs. The most important
mercenaries worked for the paramount
chief of the confederation of Bau, a
tiny island just southeast of Viti Levu.
Bau was the most powerful of the seven
confederations in Fiji during the late
nineteenth century. With the aid of
such mercenaries the Bau confederation, under the cannibal chief
Naulivou and later his brother, Tanoa,
was able to extend its influence over
most of western Fiji.

From the 1820s to about 1850 European traders began a new commercial
enterprise, the exploitation of bêche-
de-mer, the sea cucumbers which were
found throughout the islands. This new
enterprise necessitated the establish-

Fijian women display crafts,
including masi or tapa cloth
made from the inner bark of
the paper mulberry tree.

ment of processing facilities and the use of Fijian labor.

During the 1830s, the first important European settlement, Levuka on Ovalu Island off the east coast of Viti Levu, was established. The town, which grew to nearly one thousand population by the late 1800s, was the center for beachcombers, traders, whalers, copra producers, and, for a short time during the mid-1800s, cotton growers. When Fiji became a British colony in 1874, Levuka became the colony's first capital. After seven years the capital was transferred to Suva.

The Bau confederation continued to be powerful and with the rise of Chief Cakobau, the nephew of Naulivou and son of Tanoa, Fiji gained its most powerful and influential chief. By the

1850s, Cakobau's confederation ruled all of the western Fiji group, although he had many rivals — including the Tongan chief Ma'afu; chiefs in eastern Fiji, who were allies of Tonga; and rebellious leaders in Viti Levu itself. One of the most significant events during Cakobau's rule was his conversion to Christianity in 1854. This brought about great changes for Fijians, not least of which was the end of the practice of cannibalism. Christian missionaries had arrived in Fiji as early as the 1830s but it wasn't until Cakobau accepted the religion that it gained widespread acceptance. Although missionaries from a variety of Christian faiths arrived in Fiji, it was the Methodists who gained the greatest number of converts and today Methodism is the

The bure is the traditional house type of Fijians. This recently-built bure, located on the Coral Coast of Viti Levu, is occupied, but few new bure are being built today.

popular religion among native
ns. Today, a church, usually Meth-
, is found at a central location in
rural villages. Cakobau accepted
stianity at least in part to ally him-
vith the Tongans, who were al-
r Christians. By so doing, Cakobau
d the Tongans would help him put
a rebellions of lesser Fijian leaders.
use Cakobau eventually saw that
as not powerful enough to impose
ale on all of Fiji, he decided to
his kingdom to Great Britain. On
ber 10, 1874, Fiji was ceded to
en Victoria and officially became a
sh colony.

e first British colonial governor of
vas Sir Arthur Gordon, who insti-
a number of policies that had a
ng effect on the future of the
ny. Perhaps the most significant of
e was that Gordon, who saw him-
he protector of the Fijian people,
ed the sale of native land to non-
ns. Land could only be leased.
few exceptions, that law has been
ect and enforced to the present
Today, some eighty-three percent
i's land is owned by Fijians even
gh Fijians make up less than one-

half of the population. Some of the
most valuable land, however, mostly in
urban and tourist areas along the coast,
is in non-Fijian hands. Another policy
instituted by Gordon and Sir John
Thurston, his colonial secretary and
successor as governor, was the govern-
mental system of indirect rule. This was
based on the traditional Fijian chiefly
political structure and the rule that
native Fijians could not be forced to
work on plantations. Today, the Fijian
culture is among the most vibrant of
indigenous Pacific cultures and it is to
the policies of Gordon that much of the
credit for this must be given. As a result, much of the Fijian material and
non-material cultural character exists
to the present, including *yaqona* cer-
emonies, the chiefly system, and traditional housing in the form of *bures*. It is
true, however, that the strength of
such traditional material culture increases with distance from urban areas
and the major tourist regions; that is,
the more remote, rural Fijian villages
exhibit the strongest ties to the past.
Bures, for example, are no longer com-
mon in most villages as these have
been replaced by concrete block or

A rural Fijian family in the village of Matainasau in the interior of Viti Levu.

wooden houses. Some native cultural traditions, such as the fire-walking associated with the people from the island of Beqa ("Benka") and the meke — the traditional Fijian dance accompanied by song and drums — are very popular in the tourist resorts. Fijians are hired at low pay to perform these and other cultural traditions for the tourists who visit the islands.

One of the main reasons that the European powers sought colonies was, of course, for profit. One means to wealth was the establishment of plantations that produced the raw materials needed for food-processing, textile, beverage, and other industries. Such industries were almost always located in the "mother" country. Fiji was a political colony of Great Britain, but was

colonized economically more by Au tralia. Many of the largest compani Fiji were, or still are, Australian-owned. These include the Colonial Sugar Refining Company, whose h ings in Fiji were owned by Australi until 1973 when they were purchas by the Fijian government; the trad company Burns-Philip; the Morris-Hedstrom department stores found cities throughout Fiji; and the Emp Gold Mines, which controlled the Fijian gold industry for much of its istence.

The most important plantation c in Fiji, by far, was sugar cane, grow plantations in western Viti Levu ar elsewhere. Because Fijians were no required to work on the plantation and because the number of laborer ho could immigrate from other Pacific and countries, such as the Solomons, is limited by law, there was an acute ortage of laborers to work on the gar plantations. Gordon, familiar th similar labor shortage problems in e Caribbean sugar areas, saw as a ution the recruitment of indentured orers from the British colony of In-. The year 1879 is significant since vas then that the first Indian work- arrived in Fiji. The agreement was t immigrant Indian workers had to or on the plantations for five years; ing the next five-year period, these kers would be permitted to lease n Fijians small plots on which to a. After ten years they could be- e free settlers and remain on the ds, and the majority did so. Al-

though working and living conditions for Indian workers were very poor, over sixty thousand Indians made the jour- ney to Fiji between 1879 and 1916, the last year of Indian immigration. By the 1930s, many had settled on the coast of Vanua Levu to plant rice and raise goats and cows. Their descendants today compose nearly one-half of the total population of Fiji, and are pre- dominantly Hindu. Indeed, until after 1987, Indians actually outnumbered the Fijians. Today, there is an under- current of jealousy and distrust be- tween Fijians and Indians. The jealousy is related in part to the fact that Indi- ans cannot purchase and own their own land — which, to Fijians, is a sym- bol of status — while the Indians, espe- cially those living in the cities, control

ugar cane is cut and hauled from he fields in special cradling carts.

Fijians reached their homeland by water, and have remained closely tied to the ocean Here a Fijian man is at work sailing an outrigger canoe.

a disproportionate share of commercial enterprises and wealth. These tensions led to a Fijian-inspired bloodless *coup d'état* in 1987 because some Fijians were concerned that Indians might gain political control of the Fijian government following the 1987 election. Significant numbers of Indians emigrated as a result of this power struggle. Unfortunately, it was principally the well-educated professionals and wealthy who left.

On October 10, 1970, exactly ninety-six years after it became a colony of Great Britain, Fiji became fully independent nation — The Dominion of Fiji. Independence was m a response to pressure from Great B ain and other nations than to a str desire from within Fiji. Upon attair independence, Fiji established a pa mentary democracy form of govern ment and voting privileges were gi to all adults, of all races. However,

nd rights of Fijians, which had been
aranteed by the Deed of Cession in
74, were given full protection in the
nstitution. In fact, the Fijian chiefs
re given the final say on all matters
ated to the status of Fijians. In brief,
e new constitution made it clear that
ligenous Fijians would have political
wer so long as they had the support
the General Electors ("General Elec-
s" include non-Fijians and non-Indi-
, such as Europeans, part-Fijians,
l Chinese) and so long as they re-
ined unified. Lasting unity, how-
r, was not to be the case.

he nation's first prime minister was
u Sir Kamisese Mara, the leader of
the Alliance Party. The Alliance Party,
as the name suggests, was a coalition of
various groups including the Fijian As-
sociation, the Fijian Indian Alliance,
and the General Electors' Association.
A number of other political parties,
representing the views of Fijians (such
as the extremist Fijian Nationalist
Party) or Indians (such as the National
Federation Party), were also important.
In 1985, the Fiji Labor Party was
formed. It became an innovative and
major force because it represented the
large number of members of trade
unions. It was more concerned with
economic issues than racial differences.
About one year before the 1987 elec-

*The Fijian Parliament
building in Suva.*

tions, the new Labor Party formed a coalition with the National Federation Party and together they won a majority of seats in the House of Representatives (twenty-eight of fifty-two seats; nineteen of the twenty-eight coalition members were Indians), relegating the Alliance Party to minority status. Although the leader of the coalition party, Dr. Timoci Bavadra, was a native Fijian, violent protests erupted from Fijian extremists who wanted to avoid what they perceived would be domination by Indians. In May, 1987, Lieutenant Colonel Sitiveni Rabuka ("Rambuka"), the third ranking officer in Fiji's army, which comprises only ethnic Fijians, "stormed" Suva's Parliament Building with ten armed soldiers and arrested Bavadra and other coalition members. The next day, Fiji's two daily newspapers were ordered to halt publication, because they had run stories criticizing Rabuka's coup. The Governor General, Ratu Sir Penaia Ganilau, assumed control of government and attempted to effect a compromise.

With pressure and strong support from the ultra-conservative Fijians wh supported the Taukei movement, Rabuka led a second coup in September and reinstituted military rule. He then declared Fiji a republic and appointed Mara, Fiji's only previous pri minister, to that post. Among other things, Rabuka stressed the importan of traditional (Fijian) culture and Christian religious fundamentalism. Nearly all activities, including retaili entertainment (such as the cinema), and even family-centered recreation activities, were banned on Sundays. Because of their economic importan hotels and restaurants which served tourists were the exception to this b Rabuka even called for the conversi of Hindu and Moslem Fijian Indians Christianity. Although such conversions did not take place it was clear that democracy, at least for the time being, had come to an end in Fiji.

NATIONAL SYMBOLS OF FIJI

The flag of Fiji is rectangular. It has a light blue background with the red, white and dark blue British Union Jack in the upper left quadrant and the shield from the national coat of arms centered in the right half. The shield is represented in red, yellow, green, black and brown. The flag was first flown on October 10, 1970, the day that Fiji attained independence from Great Britain. Mr. Robi Wilcock and Mrs. Murray MacKenzie jointly won the competition for the design of the national flag.

The Coat of Arms of Fiji consists of a central shield; two Fijian warriors flanking the shield, with the one on the left holding a spear and the one on the right holding a war club; a Fijian canoe, called a *takia*, at the top of the shield; and the Fijian motto on a ribbon at the bottom. An heraldic lion, facing left, is at the top of the shield; it is holding a cocoa pod with its front paws. The remaining part of the shield is divided into four quadrants; from upper left clockwise, these include representations of sugar cane, coconut palms, bananas, and a dove of peace. The first three identify agricultural products important in Fiji's economy. The dove was found on the flag of Chief Cakobau's government before Fiji became a colony of Britain. The Fijian motto, *Rerevaka na Kalou ka Doka na Tui*, means "Fear God and honor the Queen."

FIJI TODAY

Today, Fiji is a Third World nation. This means that the country's population is predominantly rural, the average per capita income of its people is much lower than that found in the world's wealthy nations, the national economy is based largely on the production and export of primary commodities like sugar, timber, fish and gold, and foreign investment controls the nation's emerging manufacturing sector. In short, like poorer nations all over the globe, it is very much dependent upon the wealthy nations. Because of historical and locational considerations, Australia i. the nation upon which Fiji remains most dependent. Fiji, however, can b placed at the upper end of the Third World spectrum since most measure: economic and social characteristics reflect a higher than average standir

School children in Lutu, a rural village in interior Viti Levu.

iji. Among Pacific Island coun-
, for example, it has the highest per
:a gross national product
$1,780 in 1990). Compared to all
d World nations, Fiji has a rela-
y low young dependency ratio
) percent of the population under
:n years of age), a high life expect-
(seventy-one years), a well-edu-
d population (adult literacy rate of
eighty percent), and a relatively
: share of its population living in
n areas (forty percent).

1990, Fiji's population was esti-
:d to be nearly 736,000, a 2.9 per-
increase over the 715,375
ited in the most recent official cen-
>f August 31, 1986. At the time of
1986 national census, Indians still
esented the largest part of the
ilation, accounting for 48.7 per-
of the total population compared
ie 46.1 percent which was ethnic
n. The coups of 1987 caused large
bers of Indians to leave Fiji and by
1989 ethnic Fijians outnumbered
>-Fijians for the first time since
5. In 1990, it was estimated that
more than 360,000 ethnic Fijians
esented 48.9 percent of the total

population. Indo-Fijians in 1990 numbered nearly 340,000 (46.2 percent of
the total population), some twenty
thousand fewer than the native Fijians.
All other ethnic groups, which included Rotumans, Europeans, part-
Europeans, other Pacific Islanders, and
Chinese, numbered slightly over thirty-
six thousand (4.9 percent). In the year
and a half following the first coup of
1987, more than twelve thousand per-
sons, mostly Indians, left Fiji. Unfortunately for Fiji, these emigrants included
some seven hundred teachers and a
majority of the nation's one-hundred-
fifty lawyers and two-hundred-eighty
doctors. Such emigrants form a part of
the "brain drain" that is problematic
for most Third World nations. Most of
the professionals who left Fiji went to
developed nations of the British Commonwealth, including Australia, New
Zealand, and Canada.

According to the geographer Rajesh
Chandra, "The general ethnic environ-
ment in Fiji has encouraged the various
ethnic groups to preserve their ethnic
identities and even to develop them."
Beyond the differences in languages
and cultural traditions that continue to

Native Fijians with dalo, or taro, in the village of Matainasau, Viti Levu.

An Indo-Fijian vendor in the market at Nausori, Viti Levu.

characterize the nation's two major groups, similar "separateness" is also seen in religion since the vast majority of ethnic Fijians are Christian whereas the Indian population remains almost totally Hindu and Muslim. In 1986, 52.9 percent of the total population was Christian, 36.6 percent was Hindu, and 7.8 percent was Muslim. Among the Christians, more than two-thirds were Methodists (69.4 percent), followed by Roman Catholics (16.6 percent), Assemblies of God (4.3 percent), and Seventh Day Adventists (4.0 percent).

Most Indians in Fiji trace their ancestry to northern India but many a from other parts of that culturally di verse country. Relations among diffent Indian groups in Fiji are general excellent. Many cultural and religio traditions have been maintained by Indians; others have not. The caste system, for example, has been almos totally eliminated. The vast majorit Indo-Fijians living in Fiji were born there. Many have never been to Ind and those who do go there travel as tourists to visit the land of their anc try. One such Indo-Fijian, a retired

servant, who finally visited the
[bi]rthplace of his parents in southeast-
[ern] India informed me that, while
[ther]e, he felt very much the outsider.
[He e]ven had a difficult time making
[him]self understood because Tamil, the
[lang]uage of his ancestors, had changed
[sinc]e his parents had immigrated to Fiji
[deca]des earlier.

[Th]e separateness of the Fijians and
[Indo]-Fijians is also expressed in their
[popu]lation distribution. Generally,
[Indo]-Fijians are found either in urban
[area]s, where they work in retail busi-
[ness] and the professions, or in rural
[area]s, where they are farmers who lease
[land] in those areas where sugar cane is
[the]dominant crop. Indian farmers live
[in di]spersed farmsteads rather than in
[the]clustered settlements typical of

rural Fijians. Indeed, ninety percent of
the sugar crop is produced by Indian
farmers. In their three-room, galva-
nized metal homes, Indian farm fami-
lies enjoy a diet of *roti* — unleavened
bread — eaten with vegetable curry or,
increasingly, curry with chicken or
eggs. Cattle are kept for milk and the
production of *ghee* – rendered butter.
They also grow many vegetables for
European tastes, such as potatoes and
pumpkins; and for their own use, they
grow onions, chili peppers, mangoes,
cucumbers, radishes, and coriander –
among other specialty crops.

Fijians, on the other hand, dominate
in interior and coastal rural areas
where they live in small villages of
thirty to fifty households and tend their
livestock and fields, or "plantations,"

*An Indo-Fijian farmer plowing
with oxen in Viti Levu.*

A market scene in Suva. Yaqon root can be seen at right.

that surround the village. Most production in such plantations is subsistence crops, some of which is sold locally. Although modern foods have become increasingly important, traditional crops are still essential to village life: taro and yams are the basics, to which meat – mostly chicken and pork – and fruits are considered garnishes and treats. Many other root crops, plus coconuts, eggplants, bananas, breadfruit, and tomatoes are used in varying amounts depending on location. Coastal villagers consume a wide variety of sea life as well.

The population of Fiji is among the better-educated of Third World nations. Primary education, which includes the first eight school years (referred to as grades one to six and forms one and two), is free but not compulsory. In 1986, over ninety-four perce of the primary-aged children — tho aged six to eleven and in grades one six only — were attending one of th 672 primary schools in the country. Because of the difficulty of travel to primary schools in remote rural area school children must often stay the week in the village where their scho is located. Some parents must also s the week to help prepare meals for t children and maintain the school. Needless to say, weekends and vaca tion periods are looked forward to w anticipation!

Secondary schools usually include forms three to six, although forms o and two are sometimes included. M than forty-two thousand students at

ed the one-hundred-forty second-
chools in the nation in 1986. Un-
primary school enrollments, where
-Fijians and ethnic Fijians were
it equal, Indo-Fijians represented a
ter percentage (51.5 percent) of
secondary school enrollment than
ethnic Fijians (41.6 percent). A
oportionate share of secondary
ols are in the urban areas, making
more accessible to the Indo-
ns. Secondary schools are not free
need-based aid is available for
e who qualify. The literacy rate in
n 1986 was eighty-seven percent;
ty percent among males and
ty-four percent among females. In
lower grades, classes are taught in
mother tongue of the children
an or Hindi) and in English; as
ents progress, English becomes the
ium of instruction. Today nearly
yone in Fiji speaks English as a
nd language.

ji also has forty technical and voca-
al schools and three teacher train-
colleges. Students are trained in
ness, secretarial studies, tourism,
agriculture, among other subjects.
968, the University of the South

Pacific (USP) opened in Suva. USP is a
regional university in that it serves the
twelve South Pacific island nation-
states of Fiji, Solomon Islands, Cook
Islands, Kiribati, Tuvalu, Nauru,
Vanuatu, Niue, Tokelau, Tonga, Western Samoa, and Marshall Islands. The
University has small extension cam-
puses in most of these nations which
use satellite telecommunication link-
ages to provide higher education opportunities throughout the region. The
USP-Suva campus has about twenty-
five hundred students, the majority of
whom are Fijian citizens. There is a
separate Fiji School of Medicine in
Suva which is affiliated with USP.
Relatively affluent students go to colleges and universities outside Fiji, most
notably in Australia and New Zealand;
unfortunately, many of these students
never return to Fiji permanently.

Typical of Third World nations generally, the population of Fiji is becoming increasingly urban. Those who
work in cities find jobs in government
and other service-sector jobs and, increasingly, in manufacturing. The
"pull" of perceived employment opportunities in the cities and towns has

FIJI'S CITIES AND TOWNS
POPULATION 1966–1986

City	1966	1976	1986
Suva	87,944	125,384	162,678
Lautoka	21,221	28,847	39,057
Labasa	9,716	12,956	16,537
Nadi	11,351	12,995	15,220
Ba	8,309	9,173	10,260
Nausori	1,944	5,262	8,924
Vatukoula	4,993	6,425	4,789
Sigatoka	2,339	3,635	4,730
Rakiraki	2,708	3,755	3,361
Levuka	3,000	2,764	2,895
Savusavu	1,861	2,295	2,872
Navua	1,595	2,568	2,775
Tavua	1,994	2,144	2,227
Korovou	329	290	340
Total Urban	159,304	218,493	276,665
Total Fiji	476,727	588,068	715,375

meant that many young people have moved from rural toward urban areas. In short, high rates of rural-to-urban migration since the 1950s have meant that the populations of Fiji's cities, and most notably Suva, have grown more rapidly than those of rural areas. The urban population of Fiji increased by 26.6 percent between 1976 and 1986 whereas the population in rural areas increased by only 18.7 percent during that same period. Since population growth rates are higher for urban areas and birth rates are higher in rural ar than they are in urban areas, it is cle that Fiji is experiencing a net rural-t urban migration of people. At least three-fifths of the internal migration Fiji is rural-to-urban; about one-fiftl urban-to-rural, mostly to rural areas Ba Province, western Viti Levu; and the remaining is either urban-to-urb or rural-to-rural migration. Suva and the larger towns have grown most ra idly which suggests that people are a tracted to the bigger and better-kno aces and the employment and other opportunities that are thought to exist in those places.

Suva, the primate city of Fiji, is by far the largest. In 1986, its total metropolitan area population was more than

divided by that of the second largest.

As has been noted, Suva became Fiji's capital in 1882, replacing Levuka on tiny Ovalu Island off the eastern coast of Viti Levu. Today, Levuka is a small, sleepy port supported principally

The Population of Fiji's Cities and Towns in 1986

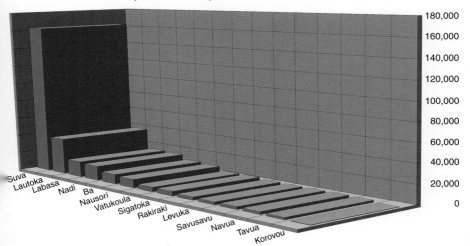

,000; the population of the city proper, "Suva City," was 69,665. Suva more than four times larger than the next largest urban place, Lautoka, the center of western Viti Levu's sugar industry. Fiji is similar to many other small and medium-sized Third World nations in that it has a high index of primacy, defined simply as the population of the largest metropolitan area

by a tuna-canning plant and a few adventuresome tourists. Suva's most rapid population growth occurred during the 1946–1956 and 1956–1966 periods when the population more than doubled each decade. The visitor to Suva finds a cosmopolitan atmosphere. Indians, Fijians, Europeans, Chinese, and other Pacific Islanders stroll the streets and shop in colorful stores that

Renwick Road, a typical mid-town street in Suva.

sell fabric, turmeric, dried fish, and betel nuts. Indian women in *saris* and Fijian men in traditional knee-length *sulu* intermingle with the short-, swimsuit-, and T-shirt-clad visitors from the other side of the world.

The recent growth in Fiji's urban population has been at least partly responsible for some of the country's urban problems — problems that can be found in cities throughout the Third World. One of these is the housing shortage that exists in Suva and in other cities and towns in Fiji. Limited public housing has been built but this is not nearly sufficient for all those in need. As a result, squatter areas have mushroomed in Suva and a few other places. This "informal" type of housing is often the only alternative for those

who have no other options. According to newspaper reports, it was estimated that ten to fifteen percent of Suva's population were squatters in the early 1980s. Some of these people may not be squatters in the strict sense of that word — for example, they may have received permission to live where they do — but they are generally very poor, lack amenities such as electricity and running water, and face health problems. Rapid increases in population and informal housing puts great strain on the existing infrastructure — roads, health facilities, schools — and make planning for future urban needs very difficult.

Perhaps the second most pressing problem facing Fiji's population is lack of employment; the growth in jobs h

Sidewalk vendors, representative of Fiji's large informal employment sector, selling sugar cane and bananas in Suva.

t kept pace with the growth of population. National unemployment rates ve increased from 4.2 percent to 6.2 rcent to 7.5 percent in the 1966, 76, and 1986 census years, respectively. Unemployment, however, is not tributed evenly throughout the nation. Two-thirds of the total unemployed were found in Fiji's urban areas d over two-fifths were in Suva alone. nsiderably more people can be classed as underemployed, and a large re of the urban labor force work is he "informal" sector, characterized n absence of regular wages or salary. Examples of jobs in the informal or include public market vendors,

sidewalk vendors, beggars, and stevedores. The formal sector, on the other hand, includes those people employed on a regular basis such as garment factory workers, civil servants, bus drivers, department store clerks, and professionals. Unemployment and the poverty that results from it give rise to undesirable outcomes such as poor health and increased crime.

As is the case in Third World nations generally, agriculture still dominates the economy of Fiji. Sugar cane, coconut products, and ginger are exported. Fruits and vegetables, such as rice, yaqona, cassava, and dalo are among the leading crops produced for local sale and subsistence. Rice is a staple among Indo-Fijians and urban populations generally, and rice-growing is strongly encouraged so that lesser amounts need to be imported. Much of the rice is produced in the southeastern part of Viti Levu. Fiji has a dairy industry centered in southern and southeastern Viti Levu, and beef and poultry are important livestock products. Agriculture, including forestry and fishing, contributed nearly one-quarter of the Gross Domestic Product (GDP) in 1990 and, according to the 1986 national census, accounted for over forty-four percent of the national labor force. Most of the sugar cane was produced by Indo-Fijians on leased land whereas native Fijians living in rural areas were mostly subsistence farmers.

Until recently, sugar was the nation leading earner of foreign revenue. In 1989, tourism surpassed sugar, and Fiji is counting on tourism to continue to be the major source of income. Fiji ha been the leader in the development o tourism among South Pacific island nation-states for the last several decades; the number of visitors to Fiji is much greater than that to the second leading tourist destination, French Polynesia (which includes Tahiti). From 1963 to 1990, gross tourism receipts rose from F$3.6 million (about US $5.3 million) to F$336 million (about US$494.9 million), and the

The Fijian tradition of firewalking, historically associated with the island of Beqa, now provides entertainment for tourists.

ism industry's share of the GDP from less than four percent in 3 to over twelve percent in 1984. number of visitors increased from over eighteen thousand in 1962 to e than one-quarter million in 1986, year before the 1987 coups. The s severely affected the tourist e so that by 1988 the number of ors declined to 208,000. In 1993, ever, the number reached an all-high of nearly 287,000. Over fifty-e hundred people were employed in s tourist industry in 1990. Unfortu-

nately, the vast majority of jobs in tourism-related activities are low-paying and require few skills.

Tourist attractions and facilities are not evenly distributed across Fiji. As the geographer Britton has pointed out, the location of tourism in Fiji has been determined by four factors which are directly linked to the impact of the colonial period: the distribution of cities; the distribution of the transportation infrastructure; the restricted availability of freehold land; and the locational priorities basic to the tourist

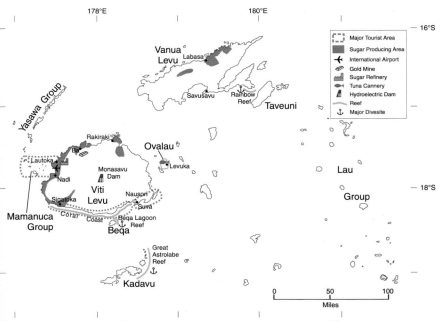

Tourism and sugar production, Fiji's most important sources of foreign revenue, are concentrated on Viti Levu and Vanua Levu.

product. As a result, the vast majority of tourist facilities and employment are located on Fiji's main island of Viti Levu, or on the nearby Yasawas, the group of small, low islands off the western coast of Viti Levu. The three major tourist areas where most of the hotels and related facilities — such as golf courses, restaurants, and souvenir shops — are located include the vicinity of the Nadi International Airport in western Viti Levu and the nearby Yasawas; the Coral Coast, a sixty-mile stretch along Viti Levu's south coast; and the Suva metropolitan area in eastern Viti Levu. Over ninety percent of international tourists, and over ninety percent of the local employment in tourism, are found in these three areas. Tourists come to Fiji for its tropical weather, beaches, coral reefs, excellent scuba diving and snorkeling, boating, and other water-related activities. It is a convenient stopover for air travelers flying from North America or Japan to Australia or New Zealand. About two-fifths of all tourists are from Australia. The next leading sources in order of importance are the United States, New Zealand, and Canada.

After tourism, it has been the manufacturing industry that has expanded most rapidly in the past few years. Like many other Third World nations, Fiji entered into what is called an import substitution industrialization (ISI) strategy following independence in 1970. The goal of such a strategy is to produce goods that will lessen the need to import those things most frequently in demand by the local population, decreasing the need to buy costly foreign-made consumer goods. Unfortunately, this strategy was not very successful since many Fijians still demanded what they perceived to be better-made and more prestigious consumer items from countries like the United States, Australia, and Japan.

More recently, the Fijian government has supported an export-oriented industrialization (EOI) strategy whereby factories that manufacture goods for export are given the highest priority. To encourage the establishment of such industries, the government in 1987 instituted a Tax Free Factory (TFF) scheme. Similar to Export Processing Zones (EPZ) in other Third World nations, the idea is to at

The Main Commodities in Fiji's Foreign Exchange, 1987–1990
in Millions of Fijian Dollars

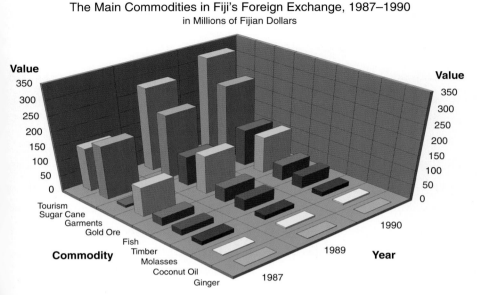

al entrepreneurs and foreign inves-
s, such as multinational corpora-
ns, to set up industries in Fiji.
nong other incentives, the govern-
nt exempted such factories from
es so long as ninety-five percent of
ir products were exported. By 1991,
re than two-hundred-fifty such fac-
es had been approved; of the one-
dred-thirteen actually imple-
ted, over sixty-five percent were
ment factories. Other export-ori-
d industries that are expected to
v are those that produce furniture
other wood products and those
make footwear. Just under one-

half of the factories in operation are
locally-owned and the rest are either
foreign-owned or owned jointly by foreign and local investors. About three-
quarters of the foreign investment is by
Australians or New Zealanders.

The principal source of imports to
Fiji is Australia, which accounted for
nearly one-third of all imports in 1990.
The next most important source na-
tions were New Zealand, the United
States, and Japan. The principal mar-
ket for Fijian exports is the United
Kingdom, which accounted for more
than one-third of all exports in 1990.
Australia was the second leading desti-

nation for exports with over one-fifth of the total. The most important imports by value in 1990 were manufactured goods and miscellaneous manufactured items (thirty-two percent of the total) and machinery and transportation equipment (thirty-one percent of the total). Because Fiji produces no fossil fuels, it must import all of its fossil fuel needs. Mineral fuels accounted for over fourteen percent of the imports by value in 1990. This would have been more except that the government has developed much of the considerable hydroelectric potential of the nation. In 1983, the Monasavu project, located in interior Viti Levu, began operating and is today Fiji's principal power source.

Fiji has consistently recorded a trade deficit and, in 1990, it was estimated that the deficit was in excess of F$250 million. However, net receipts from tourism, official aid and development assistance from other nations, and other income meant that the total national budget showed a deficit of "only F$40 million for 1990.

Transportation is reasonably well developed on Viti Levu but much less developed on the other islands. The country has over twenty-five hundred

Fiji's Principal Trading Partners, 1990
Thousands of Fijian Dollars

Nation	Imports	Exports
Australia	308,595	122,038
New Zealand	180,797	88,047
United States	143,579	55,041
Japan	122,500	42,757
Singapore	64,505	22,371
Taiwan	44,192	13,580
United Kingdom	33,494	211,641
Hong Kong	32,081	4,923
People's Republic of China	30,891	3,884
West Germany	17,669	1,780
India	9,068	0
Other Pacific Countries	2,937	42,250
Total	990,308	608,312

iles of roads, but only about fifteen ercent of the road system was paved the early 1980s. One of the most aveled highways in Fiji is Queen's oad, which hugs the south coast of iti Levu and connects Lautoka and adi with Suva and Nausori. Queen's oad, nearly all of which is paved, sses through the Coral Coast area, e of Fiji's major tourist areas and also sses through or near the towns of ̩atoka, Navua, and Pacific Harbor, latter a tourist development which ludes two first-class hotels and hous- for wealthy Fijians and foreigners. ̩ific Harbor has one of the few ex- sive sandy beaches on Viti Levu. ̩g's Road, the route around the thern portion of Viti Levu, com- ̩es the three-hundred-mile circle und the island. Most of the King's ̩d is now paved which makes for a ̩fortable and scenic drive near or ̩g the north coast. Bus service is ly available and the bus fares are reasonable. ̩i has an extensive inter-island air ̩m served mainly by Air Fiji. Air ̩fic is Fiji's international airline like all international flights, lands

at and departs from Nadi in western Viti Levu; thus, those travelers whose destination is Suva must either fly to Nausori or take the two to four hour drive by bus, taxi, or car to Suva via Queen's Road. A third inter-island carrier, Sunflower Airlines, links Nadi with a number of out-of-the-way places. Even Rotuma, Fiji's most re- mote populated island, is served by air twice a week.

Fiji has a well-developed inter-island shipping network carrying cargo and passengers, although fewer passengers are traveling by boat as inter-island air service increases. Many of the smaller islands, however, can only be reached by ferries, copra boats, or other inter- island cargo vessels. Suva is the major port and Lautoka and Levuka are also ports-of-call. Over eight hundred ships call at Suva each year, including a number of passenger liners and cruise ships.

With the exception of the Fiji Sugar Corporation Railway which is used during the sugar cane harvesting sea- son, the country has no passenger rail- way system.

Following the political turmoil that

Fishing boats and nets along an estuary on northern Viti Levu, just off King's Road.

resulted in the two coups of 1987, ethnic Fijians today are firmly in control. A new constitution for the Sovereign Democratic Republic of Fiji was promulgated in July, 1990, which declared that Fiji was a democratic republic and guaranteed fundamental human rights and equality before the law for all its citizens. Having said that, it also is true that the new constitution seeks to affirm that the political control of the country is in the hands of the Fijian elite. For example, certain positions — Prime Minister, President, certain ministers, and others — will always be held by Fijians irrespective of the outcome of the elections. Ethnic Fijians and Polynesian Rotumans receive special consideration in the constitution, including positive discrimination for em-

ployment in government jobs and in the legal system. The constitution als exonerates all those who participated in the 1987 coups. The Great Counc of Chiefs — *Bose Levu Vakaturaga* — appoints the President and selects th twenty-four (of thirty-four total) Fiji nominees to the Senate, the upper chamber of the Parliament. The Hou of Representatives is the lower cham ber of Parliament; its seventy membe are elected. However, thirty-seven seats are reserved for ethnic Fijians, twenty-seven seats for Indo-Fijians, one for a Rotuman, and five seats fo other races — the General Electors.

The 1987 coups had a major impa on Fiji's external relations. Until th time, Fiji had been a member of the British Commonwealth of Nations a ad especially close links to Australia, New Zealand, and India. After 1987, those links deteriorated significantly. Given the very negative effect of the coups on the Indo-Fijian population, it was to be expected that India would become a major critic of the new authoritarian regime. As a result of criticism by the Indian government, the Fijian government ordered the end of diplomatic relations with India in 1990. The Commonwealth nations also criticized Fiji's new constitution and in 1991 stated that Fiji would not be readmitted to the Commonwealth until its constitution was changed. Fiji's foreign economic policies, however, are still closely aligned with those nations with which it has historic ties. Thus, Australia and New Zealand are still major trading partners and provide Fiji with most of its visitors. Fiji has made efforts to cultivate ties with Southeast Asia, and new investment and trade data show that these efforts are bearing fruit. Increasingly, other Pacific Rim nations and especially the United States and Japan figure to become major players in Fiji's future.

Fiji belongs to most regional organizations including the South Pacific Forum, the South Pacific Commission, the United Nation's Economic and Social Commission for Asia and the Pacific (ESCAP), and the South Pacific Regional Trade and Economic Cooperative Agreement (SPARTECA).

In Fiji, as is true for most South Pacific tropical island nations, environmental concerns loom large because the amount of land is so limited. Those environmental issues most pressing to Fijians, and to most other Pacific Islanders, are global warming; loss of ocean resources, including fisheries and coral reefs; nuclear testing and its aftermath; the loss of forest cover, mangroves, and other natural vegetation and fauna and land degradation; and natural hazards, especially destructive tropical storms.

The predicted increase in global temperature causes great concern among many because this will ultimately lead to the melting of ice in high latitudes and thus rising sea levels all over the globe. Clearly, rising sea levels would affect all islands to some degree and the low islands, such as atolls, could disappear beneath the sea altogether.

A young Fijian preparing fish on Dravuni.

International conferences have been held in the Pacific region to address this issue and Australia has taken the lead in the monitoring and scientific study of regional climatic change and the environmental consequences of global warming. Decreasing ozone levels associated with the "hole" in the ozone layer over Antarctica, while not yet of major concern to Fijians, could become so.

Fisheries resources throughout the Pacific have been depleted by the large fishing fleets of Japan, Korea, Taiwan, and the United States. Such nations have often ignored maritime boundaries and the oceanic resources claimed by the small nations of the region. Furthermore, fishing practices such as the use of very long drift nets for tuna fish-

ing have very negative consequences for marine resources. Drift net fishing catches everything, especially when nets greater than a mile in length are used. Tourism and pollutants, such a chemical runoff from the use of fertilizer, are of potential harm to the cora reefs.

Because of its "emptiness," several the world's nuclear powers saw the Pacific as a place to test their newly-developed bombs. The United State tested atomic bombs on tiny islands possessed in Micronesia. Thus, Bikir and Enewetok were test sites; an atomic bomb was first tested on Bik in 1946 and the first hydrogen bom was tested there in 1954. The Unite States no longer uses Pacific islands such purposes, but France does. Fur ore, the perception of the Pacific ast empty area has been used by rge powers to justify the idea of gion becoming a dumping ground zardous wastes. For example, the d States recently used its John-Atoll as a disposal area for chemi-eapons. Fiji has not been a ar test site or dumping ground for dous wastes, but as a leader g the small nations of the region become very concerned about t may be affected. For example, rganization called the Nuclear-and Independent Pacific was led in Fiji in 1975 and continues rk toward the goal identified in its . Finally, it is worth noting that fter-effects of environmental di-

sasters like Chernobyl have been noticed by Pacific islanders.

Other people-made environmental problems that have emerged are related to degradation of the land, soils, and flora and fauna. The introduction of plantation crops such as sugar cane during the colonial period and the increasing pressures created by the growing human populations are but two of the reasons that Fiji's natural environments, including its offshore reefs and fisheries, are threatened. Rainforests, sea turtles, iguanas, and a variety of endemic bird species are a few examples of flora and fauna that have been severely affected by the clearing of natural vegetation and overfishing.

Growing population and economic development is transforming the landscape of Fiji. Forest clearing has extended across the coastal plain and up the lower slopes of mountains, while drainage ditches carry away excess water.

A RETURN TO TRADITION

We are in a time when phrases like "shrinking world" and "global economy" are much in use. These terms mean that the world is becoming increasingly interconnected, and it is useful to examine Fiji's future in the context of such a world. Which contemporary patterns and processes, both those that appear to be internal (unique) to Fiji as well as those that are external, are of relevance to Fiji's future? Three seem most important, in light of what has already been said.

First, an internal issue that Fiji must resolve is the difference that exists between its two largest population groups, the native Fijians and Indo-Fijians. The new constitution does not give equal political opportunities to native Fijians and Indo-Fijians and, until both groups are treated equally, little change in ethnic relations and relative status can be expected. We have seen how central the chiefly system, communal land ownership, and political control

are to the way of life of native Fijia Not surprisingly, all other racial gr in Fiji also aspire to owning land ar having equal political status, but in most do not have such opportuniti The academician, Jagmohan, has summed up the problem as follows: seems to me that one of the greate obstacles facing (ethnic) Fijians to is the(ir) failure to recognize that t is a contradiction; they must now r the momentous choice between pr serving and changing their 'way of The belief that they can do both si taneously is a monstrous nonsense which they have been straddled for many years now that its eradicatio may be very difficult to achieve." C unfortunate way that this issue is b resolved is through the emigration its citizens, including the best-educ people in Fiji. In the long term, a n racial democracy is what is needed a peaceful and stable Fiji, but clear that condition does not exist at the ent time.

second major issue of Fiji's future
lves around the characteristics of
country's economy, whose origins
be traced to the nineteenth cen-
and the colonial period. Fiji's
nomy is not very diversified — it
depended upon a very few products
xport, mostly primary commodi-
and on relatively few foreign mar-
. The most important commodities
orically have been sugar, coconut
lucts, and gold, and more recently
ber, fish, and a few minor agricul-
l crops like ginger. Australia and
Zealand have been Fiji's most
ortant foreign markets.

recent years the economy has ex-
led so that tourism and garment
ufacturing have become important

earners of foreign revenue as well. It
appears that these industries will ex-
pand further in the near future as the
Fijian government has encouraged
growth in these sectors through a number of incentives. Unfortunately, most
employment that is derived from tourism and garment manufacturing is low-
paying and low-skilled, providing very
little real improvement in standard of
living of the workforce. While Fiji is an
"upper echelon" Third World nation in
terms of most of the standard measures
of economic development, there is also
considerable evidence to suggest that
poverty in Fiji has increased in recent
years. Furthermore, much of the tourism and manufacturing is a result of
foreign investment, sometimes by huge
multinational corporations that have

*The harbor at Lautoka, with
Fiji's major sugar refinery in the
background. Sugar probably will
remain an important source of
income for Fiji into the near
future.*

larger budgets than the host nation wherein their factory is located. In a capitalist world such as ours, where profit is a major motivator, such foreign investment can leave a country like Fiji as quickly as it arrived, especially when profits are likely to be greater else- where. Fiji needs to continue to seek ways to diversify further its economy and its markets.

A third issue that continues to be highly relevant to Fiji's future is its geographical location in the world and the environmental challenges related to such a location. On the one hand, the world is shrinking in a relative sense as technological advancements in transportation and telecommunications bring places "closer together," or at least allow people to become much more familiar with different cultures, consumption patterns, and new ideas. On the other hand, technological changes in transport, such as newer and much faster jet aircraft able to fly farther without refueling, have also meant that small (and to some, unim-

portant) places in "empty" areas lik the South Pacific will be ignored ar become even more marginalized tha they have been in the past. The sh ing world notion also has facilitated emigration from places like Fiji to, example, Australia and the United States, where much greater econom opportunities are perceived to exist Thus, such places could slowly becc depopulated, especially by those wh Fiji can least afford to lose. Finally, changes in the global physical envir ment — notably climate change an earthquakes or volcanoes which ha not affected Fiji in recent times, bu could, given its location near a tect plate boundary — could wreak hav on small island nations.

Movement toward a truly multi-r cial democracy, coupled with contir ued diversification of both the eco- nomic base and foreign markets, sh help Fiji become better connected t the global economy and therefore le marginalized in the decades ahead.

Tourism, based on tropical climate and traditional culture, is now the most impor source of foreign revenue for Fiji. Here, a coconut climber performs for tourists alon, Coral Coast of Viti L

GEOGRAPHICAL MILESTONES
in Fijian History

1500 BC	First wave of Polynesians arrived in Fiji.
ca. 500 BC	Melanesians reached and settled Fiji Islands.
AD 1643	Abel Tasman became first European to sight Fiji Islands.
1789	Captain William Bligh, following mutiny on the *Bounty*, sailed through Fiji Islands and provided first-hand description.
1804	Sandalwood trade began, initiating Western economic interest in Fiji, and lasted about ten years.
1830s	Levuka, on Ovalu Island, became site of first important European settlement in Fiji; first Christian missionaries arrive.
1846	First United States consulate established in Fiji.
1854	Cakobau, most powerful Fijian chief of his time, converted to Christianity.
1860s	First sugar cane planted in Fiji late in decade; sugar became Fiji's most important source of revenue for decades.
1874	Fiji declared a British colony with capital at Levuka; Sir Arthur Gordon appointed first colonial governor.
1875	Measles epidemic killed approximately 40,000 native Fijians, nearly one fourth of the population.
1879	First shipload of Indian sugar workers arrived in Fiji.
1881	Capital transferred from Levuka to Suva; Rotuma and its dependencies added to Fiji territory.
1916	Indian immigration ended.
1920	Indentured labor program bringing Indians to Fiji ended.
1940	Native Land Trust Board established.
1946	For the first time, based on 1946 census, Indo-Fijians outnumbered native Fijians.
1970	Fiji granted independence on October 10.
1987	Two coups, led by Lieutenant Colonel Sitiveni Rabuka, resulted in overthrow of elected government and onset of emigration of Indians.
1989	Native Fijians again became the most numerous ethnic group, following the onset of Indo-Fijian emigration.
1990	New constitution promulgated.
1992	Major General Sitiveni Rabuka became Prime Minister.

Sources of
ADDITIONAL INFORMATION

LITERATURE

Britton, S. G. 1980. "The Spatial Organization of Tourism in a Neo-Colonial Economy: A Fiji Case Study." *Pacific Viewpoint*, volume 21 (2): 144–165.

Chandra, R., and J. Bryant (editors). 1990. *Population of Fiji*. Nouemea, New Caledonia: South Pacific Commission.

Gmohan, M. 1993. "Fighting Back." *Pacific Islands Monthly*, volume 63 (February): 32–34.

Say, R. 1990. *Fiji: A Travel Survival Kit*. Berkeley, CA: Lonely Planet Publications.

Schütz, A. J. 1979. *Say it in Fijian. An Entertaining Introduction to the Language of Fiji*. Brisbane, Australia: Robert Brown & Associates.

Stanley, D. 1990. *Fiji Islands Handbook*. Second edition. Chico, CA: Moon Publications, Inc.

Sturton, M., and A. McGregor. 1991. *Fiji: Economic Adjustment, 1987-91*. Honolulu, HI: Pacific Islands Development Program, East-West Center, Economic Report No. 1.

Ward, R. G. 1989. "Earth's Empty Quarter? The Pacific Islands in a Pacific Century." *The Geographical Journal*, volume 155 (2: July): 235-246.

IMPORTANT ADDRESSES

Embassy of Fiji
2233 Wisconsin Avenue, NW, Suite 240
Washington, DC 20007
Telephone: 202-337-8320

Fiji Visitors Bureau
5777 West Century Boulevard, Suite 220
Los Angeles, California 90045
Telephone: 310-568-1616

FIJI
at a Glance

Official Name	The Sovereign Democratic Republic of Fiji.
Derivation of the Name	From the Tongan word *Viti*, the name for the main Fiji Islands
Short Name	Fiji
Official Flag	Light blue background with Fiji coat of arms nearly centered on right half of flag and British Union Jack occupying upper left quadrant of flag.
National Anthem	*God Bless Fiji*
Form of Government	Republic, with a constitution, president, prime minister, cabinet, and a two-house Parliament, with an appointed Senate and elected House of Representatives. The hereditary Council of Chiefs retains much separate political control.
Term for Citizens	Fijians
Area	7,056 square miles
Population	715,375 (1986 census); 805,000 (estimated 1994)
Percent Urban	40
Official Language	English
National Capital	Suva
Most Populous City	Suva (1986: city proper – 69,665; metropolitan area – 162,678)
Currency	Fiji Dollar (0.68 F$ = 1 US$ in 1994)
Mean Annual Income	Per capita GNP = US$1,780 (1990)
National Motto	*Rerevaka na Kalou ka Doka na Tui* ("Fear God and honor the Queen")
Dominant Ethnic Groups	Fijian (48.9%); Indo-Fijian (46.2%)
Dominant Religions	Christianity (53%); Hinduism (37%); Islam (8%)
National Holidays	January 1 (New Year's Day); Good Friday; Easter; May 30 (Ratu Sir Lala Subuna Day); June 13 (Queen's Birthday); July 25 (Constitution Day); August 15 (Prophet Muhammed's Birthday); October 10 (Fiji Independence Day); November 3 (Diwali Day); December 25 (Christmas Day); December 26 (Boxing Day).
National Sports	Rugby, cricket, field hockey, soccer